Life As ...

Life As a Child in a apanese Internment Camp

Laura L. Sullivan

Cavendish Square

New York

Published in 2017 by Cavendish Square Publishing, LLC
243 5th Avenue, Suite 136, New York, NY 10016

Website: cavendishsq.com

This publication represents the opinions and views of the author based on his or her personal experience, knowledge, and research. The information in this book serves as a general guide only. The author and publisher have used their best efforts in preparing this book and disclaim liability rising directly or indirectly from the use and application of this book.

CPSIA Compliance Information: Batch #CS16CSQ

All websites were available and accurate when this book was sent to press.

Library of Congress Cataloging-in-Publication Data

Names: Sullivan, Laura L., 1974- author.
Title: Life as a child in a Japanese internment camp / Laura L. Sullivan.
Description: New York : Cavendish Square Publishing, [2016] | Series: Lifeas... | Includes index. | Description based on print version record and CIP data provided by publisher; resource not viewed.
Identifiers: LCCN 2015048707 (print) | LCCN 2015048512 (ebook) | ISBN 9781502617705 (ebook) | ISBN 9781502617927 (pbk.) | ISBN 9781502617828 (library bound) | ISBN 9781502617637 (6 pack)
Subjects: LCSH: Japanese Americans--Evacuation and relocation, 1942-1945--Juvenile literature. | World War, 1939-1945—Children—United States—Juvenile literature.
Classification: LCC D769.8.A6 (print) | LCC D769.8.A6 S85 2016 (ebook) | DDC 940.53/1773083--dc23
LC record available at http://lccn.loc.gov/2015048707

Editorial Director: David McNamara
Editor: Kristen Susienka
Copy Editor: Rebecca Rohan
Art Director: Jeffrey Talbot
Designer: Alan Sliwinski
Senior Production Manager: Jennifer Ryder-Talbot
Photo Research: J8 Media

Printed in the United States of America

Contents

Introduction

In 1941, the United States entered World War II by declaring war on Japan. This decision was made after Japan bombed a naval base in Hawaii. Soon after, many US citizens became afraid of the Japanese Americans living in their country. Most of the Japanese Americans had lived in the United States for years, and many were citizens, but some people worried that they might be loyal to Japan. In response to these fears, most Japanese Americans living on the west coast of the United States were forced to live in **internment camps**. They left behind their belongings, homes, and jobs. Because of this, many lives were changed forever.

Japanese-American children and their families were sent to internment camps after the US entered World War II.

WESTERN DEFENSE COMMAND AND FOURTH ARMY
WARTIME CIVIL CONTROL ADMINISTRATION

Presidio of San Francisco, California
May 23, 1942

INSTRUCTIONS
TO ALL PERSONS OF
JAPANESE
ANCESTRY
Living in the Following Area:

All of that portion of the County of Santa Clara, State of California, lying generally north and northwest of the following boundary: Beginning at the point on the Santa Cruz-Santa Clara County line, due west of a line drawn through the peak of Loma Prieta; thence due east along said line through said peak to its intersection with Llagas Creek; thence downstream along said creek toward Madrone to the point where it is crossed by Llagas Avenue; thence northeasterly on Llagas Avenue to U. S. Highway No. 101; thence northerly on said Highway No. 101 to Cochran Road; thence northeasterly on Cochran Road to its junction with Steeley Road; thence easterly on Steeley Road to Madrone Springs; thence along a line projected due east from Madrone Springs to its intersection with the Santa Clara-Stanislaus County line; together with all portions of Santa Clara County not previously covered by Exclusion Orders of this Headquarters.

Pursuant to the provisions of Civilian Exclusion Order No. 96, this Headquarters, dated May 23, 1942, all persons of Japanese ancestry, both alien and non-alien, will be evacuated from the above area by 12 o'clock noon, P. W. T., Saturday, May 30, 1942.

No Japanese person will be permitted to move into, or out of, the above area after 12 o'clock noon, P. W. T., Saturday, May 23, 1942, without obtaining special permission from the representative of the Commanding General, Northern California Sector, at the Civil Control Station located at:

> Men's Gymnasium,
> San Jose State College,
> 4th and San Carlos Streets,
> San Jose, California.

Such permits will only be granted for the purpose of uniting members of a family, or in cases of grave emergency.

The Civil Control Station is equipped to assist the Japanese population affected by this evacuation in the following ways:

1. Give advice and instructions on the evacuation.
2. Provide services with respect to the management, leasing, sale, storage or other disposition of most kinds of property, such as real estate, business and professional equipment, household goods, boats, automobiles and livestock.
3. Provide temporary residence elsewhere for all Japanese in family groups.
4. Transport persons and a limited amount of clothing and equipment to their new residence.

The Following Instructions Must Be
1. A responsible member of each family, p
the property is held, and each individual livi
instructions. This must be done between 8:00
and 5:00 P. M. on Monday, May 25, 1942.

2. Evacuees must carry with them on departure for the Assembly Center, the following property:
(a) Bedding and linens (no mattress) for each member of the family;
(b) Toilet articles for each member of the family;
(c) Extra clothing for each member of the family;
(d) Essential personal effects for each member of the family.

Chapter 1
America Enters World War II

Before World War II, thousands of Japanese people moved to the United States. Most settled on the west coast. They farmed or opened small businesses, and they were eager to succeed in their new home. Some white Americans thought the Japanese Americans were competing for jobs. They passed new laws that made it harder for Japanese people to move to the United States, become citizens, or own property.

World War II began in 1939 when Germany invaded Poland. Eventually, the English, French, Americans, and Russians fought the Germans, Italians, and Japanese. The United States entered the war after Japan attacked Pearl Harbor, Hawaii, on December 7, 1941.

Pearl Harbor

The attack on Pearl Harbor was a total surprise. Hundreds of Japanese warplanes bombed US ships and planes. In less than two hours, 2,390 Americans were killed in the attack and 1,178 were wounded. Many ships were damaged, although all but three could be repaired. (They were later used in the war.) Japan believed this attack on Pearl Harbor would keep America out of the war. It had the opposite effect. President Roosevelt declared war the next day.

After that, many people did not trust Japanese Americans. There was no evidence that they were dangerous, but many people formed racial **prejudice**.

On February 19, 1942, President Franklin D. Roosevelt signed an order outlining "military areas" where Japanese Americans couldn't live. Soon, thousands of Japanese Americans were rounded up and forced to live in camps. These camps were places where Japanese Americans were kept, or interned, until the war was over. They were called internment camps.

Each family was given a number and had to wear identification tags.

Mochida

Chapter 2
Torn From Home

By April 1942, Japanese families were told they would have to go to internment camps. Some were only given a few days to get ready. Each person could take only what they could carry. A family might have to sell their house and furniture, or beg their neighbors to look after their farm while they were gone. Almost everything they owned was left behind.

Each family was given a number. It was pinned to their clothes and their luggage. Then, the families were sent to one of many camps. They had no idea what would happen to them or if they would ever return to their old lives.

The camps were mostly located in dry, hot, and isolated places. There were several kinds of camps.

At first, **internees** were sent to temporary camps run by the military. Later, they went to permanent camps. These were run by civilian, or non-military, groups.

Japanese Americans by the Numbers

In 1942, there were about 127,000 Japanese Americans in the United States. Of that number, about 112,000 lived on the west coast. About 80,000 were second-generation (*nisei*) or third-generation (*sansei*) residents. They had been born in the United States and were US citizens. The rest were *issei*, who were born in Japan and later moved to the United States. However, anyone with Japanese ancestry could be interned, even if they had been born in the United States and lived there all their lives. Even someone who was one-sixteenth Japanese—meaning one great-great-grandparent was Japanese—could be interned.

The internment camps were located in distant, lonely places.

Farewell to Manzanar

Jeanne Wakatsuki Houston, a Japanese American born in California, was seven when her family was forced to relocate to the Manzanar internment camp. The camp was in the middle of the desert. The rooms were very crowded, the food was terrible, and there were no walls between the toilets. As an adult, Houston wrote a book about her experiences in the internment camp. It is called *Farewell to Manzanar*.

All children in the internment camps attended school.

Chapter 3

Life in an Internment Camp

Both adults and children were relocated. There were at least thirty thousand Japanese-American children in the **detention** facilities. Though they had many difficulties, there was an effort to make their lives as normal as possible. All of the children went to school. Many played sports or joined clubs. Their parents were offered jobs, mostly farming or maintenance work, for very low pay. Despite these things, the Japanese Americans were still prisoners.

Schools were built in all of the camps. However, schoolrooms were very small and crowded. Most did not have enough books or school supplies for the students. There was also a teacher shortage. Classes might have nearly fifty students for every teacher. Though the

Baseball was a popular activity in the camps, for both adults and children.

schools taught all of the usual subjects, lessons usually focused on **democracy** and loyalty to America.

Sports helped both children and adults forget their unpleasant situation for a while. Baseball was especially popular because it was such an American sport. Most internment camps eventually had a baseball diamond. Other popular sports included football, basketball,

Daily Life

6–7 a.m.	Eat breakfast in mess hall
7:30 a.m.	Line up for first count of all internees
7:45 a.m.	Line up for school
8 a.m.	Start school
11:30–12:30	Eat lunch
3 p.m.	End school day
3–4:30 p.m.	Play sports, do crafts, or play with friends
4:45 p.m.	Line up for dinner
5–6 p.m.	Eat dinner
6:30 p.m.	Line up for second count of all internees
7 p.m.	Study
8:30 p.m.	Go to bed

Meals were served in buildings called mess halls. Sometimes the food wasn't very good.

softball, and volleyball. Kids and adults could also practice traditional Japanese martial arts.

No matter how normal the people in charge tried to make everyday life, the camps were still a kind of prison. Most of them were surrounded by barbed wire.

There were armed guards. Internees were constantly counted. A lot of time was spent lining up—for roll call, for the bathroom, or for dinner.

Food was served in large cafeterias called mess halls. There were many complaints about the food. At first, the internees had to eat foods they weren't used to, like hot dogs and potatoes. Later, they were given more traditional Japanese food. Rice was common, and many meals included pickled vegetables called *tsukemono*.

The internment camps were huge prison cities where entire families lived under guard.

Chapter 4

Making a Home in Prison

When Japanese-American families were forced to move to internment camps, they left most of their possessions behind. As the months (and years) passed and they remained in the camps, many people turned to their own knowledge and creativity to make the things that were missing in their lives.

Though every internee was fed, certain foods were scarce. Especially in the first year, fresh meat was hard to find. Fruits and vegetables came from cans instead of being fresh. Later, though, the internees began to raise

Internees lived in crowded barracks with very little privacy.

Internees created beautiful works of art.

their own cows and sheep for meat. They also farmed, though most of the camps were in hot places where crops were difficult to grow.

Japanese-American internees lived in overcrowded **barracks**. A room meant for six people might actually house twenty. With so little privacy, internees soon learned to create room dividers from scrap wood. They built shelves or drawers to hold their personal items.

But function wasn't the only thing on the minds of the internees. Japanese culture places great emphasis on the appreciation of beauty. There was little beauty to be found in the internment camps. Many of the internees created their own beauty. Creating art and crafts helped the internees pass time and gave them a way to express themselves.

Art From the Camps

When the war ended, much of the art made by the internees was left behind. Some of these things have become collectors' items, but that has created controversy. The objects belong to the people who made them. Some argue that it is not right that other people are profiting from internees' art. In 2015, an auction house planned to sell four hundred pieces made by Japanese-American internees. After strong public protest, the auction was canceled. Though it might not be possible to trace the original artists, the objects will likely go to a museum. That way, people today can better understand what life was like in an internment camp.

The internment of Japanese Americans caused much suffering.

Chapter 5

The Legacy of the Internment Camps

Following the bombing of Pearl Harbor, the US government reacted in a way that it officially regrets today. Even though most intelligence showed that there was little threat from the Japanese-American population in the United States, racism and fear led to thousands of families being imprisoned.

After the war ended in 1945, there were efforts to make things right. In 1976, President Gerald Ford admitted that the imprisonment of Japanese Americans was a "national mistake." In 1988, the US government officially apologized for the treatment of Japanese Americans during this time. Each camp survivor was paid $20,000. Though nothing could make up for the years of their lives that were taken from them or the loss of their possessions and livelihood, the money sent the important message that the United States had acted wrongly.

Today, many internment camps are preserved as national historic sites. Many people visit the camps every year to learn more about them. Families and schools take trips to the camps. They can see what it was like to live there during the war, and imagine the daily life of a man, woman, or child. Some survivors and their families have even reunited there to tour the camps and share memories of their imprisonment.

Today, many of the children who lived in the camps have grown up. Some of the children have become teachers, scientists, actors, and engineers. They are changing the world and making a difference in their communities, even though they once faced difficult times living in the United States.

Though their lives were torn apart, many former internees have gone on to have success.

Glossary

barracks Buildings used to house soldiers or large numbers of people.

democracy A kind of government in which the people hold the power, usually by voting for representatives.

detention Keeping a person confined or in custody.

internee A person who lives in an internment camp.

internment camp A prison camp in which suspected people are kept during wartime.

prejudice Dislike of a group because of their race or other characteristics.

Find Out More

Books

Bailey, Rachel A. *The Japanese Internment Camps*. Ann Arbor, MI: Cherry Lake Publishing, 2014.

Oppenheim, Joanne. *Dear Miss Breed: True Stories of the Japanese Incarceration During World War II and the Librarian Who Made a Difference*. New York: Scholastic, 2006.

Website

Our Story: Life in a World War II Japanese American Internment Camp

amhistory.si.edu/ourstory/activities/internment

Video

***Children of the Camps*. Directed by Satsuki Ina, PhD.**

www.pbs.org/cOhildofcamp/documentary

Index

Page numbers in **boldface** are illustrations. Entries in **boldface** are glossary terms.

About the Author

Laura L. Sullivan is the author of more than thirty fiction and nonfiction books for children, including the fantasies *Under the Green Hill* and *Guardian of the Green Hill*. She has written many books for Cavendish Square, including *Life As a Cowboy in the American West, Life As a Spy in the American Revolution, Life As an Explorer with Lewis and Clark,* and *Life As a Passenger on the Mayflower.*